Poisonous Mushrooms
of
Alaska

Judy Hall Jacobson

Windy Ridge Publishing
P.O. Box 1158
Haines, Alaska 99827
(907) 314- 0111

© 2014 by Judy Hall Jacobson

"There are old mushroom hunters,

and bold mushroom hunters, but

there are few old, bold mushroom

hunters."

Above: Deadly Galerina   Cover photos: Clock-
wise from top: Alcohol Inky, The Sickener,
Purple Staining Bearded Milk Cap, Fly Agaric.
Title page: Clustered Collybia.

Table of Contents

Introduction

Fortunately, deadly poisonous mushrooms are not as common in Alaska and the Yukon as they can be in other places. We do have several and some resemble well-known species of wild edible mushrooms. To prevent mushroom poisoning, mushroom gatherers must familiarize themselves with the mushrooms they collect to eat, as well as with any similar-looking toxic species.

To dispel mycophobia, here are the stats: Fifty percent of mushrooms are inedible; either too tough, like most woody shelf fungi, indigestible, or too small to consider eating. Twenty-five percent are edible, but not all that incredible. You can eat them without ill effects, but they either don't taste good or are tasteless. Twenty percent will make you sick by irritating your digestive tract. In mild cases, you may throw up. In more severe cases, your digestive tract expels whatever is bothering it, in whatever direction is quickest. In severe cases, this effect continues for several days. Four percent are tasty to excellent. A mere one percent of mushrooms contain toxins that can kill you.

There are eight major groups of toxins:

1. AMANITIN

Amanitin is a toxic peptide produced by some mushrooms. It inhibits the RNA polymerase. RNA polymerase enzymes are essential to life and found in all organisms.

Amanitin poisoning is the worst mushroom poisoning you can experience. Its fatality rate is around 50%. Species that produce this toxin cause more deaths around the planet than all other poisonous wild mushrooms combined. The main culprits of this poisoning are the Death Cap (*Amanita phalloides*) and the Destroying Angel (*A. virosa/A. bisporigera*). These species, while not reported in Alaska, may make their way here through, for instance, gardening materials.

A "little brown mushroom" ("aka LBM,") such as the Deadly Galerina (*Galerina marginata*) does contain Amanitin and is common in Alaska. The death cap mushroom is far more lethal than *Galerina marginata*. The lethal dose for the death cap is around two ounces (fresh weight). For the Deadly Galerina, a healthy human adult would need to eat about twenty caps for it to be to be fatal. Obviously, Deadly Galerina, should not be eaten in any quantity. It resembles the edible species *Kuehneromyces mutabilis.*

Symptoms take up to 24 hours after the poisonous mushrooms are consumed, to show up. Unfortunately, this gives the body time to absorb the toxins. Diagnosis is a problem since, by the time the symptoms show up, there may not be uneaten specimens left for identification. Symptoms that can be mistaken for influenza or a stomach virus, include nausea, vomiting, abdominal cramps and diarrhea.

A period of improvement (the honeymoon) lasts approximately 24 hours. A misdiagnosed patient released from medical supervision returns home only to experience liver and kidney failure resulting in coma, permanent debilitating liver/kidney damage and death.

Drugs such as penicillin, activated charcoal and electrolytes, are used in some cases. The only option for victims of these poisonous wild mushrooms is a liver transplant. Many victims never fully recover from permanent organ damage.

2. GASTROINTESTINAL IRRITANTS

These are the most common forms of mushroom poisoning but -- fortunately -- the least troublesome. Mushrooms contain many different proteins and amino acids, some of which are found only in certain species or genera of mushrooms. They can cause mild to severe gastrointestinal irritation. Identification of the active ingredients is not often done perhaps because they are seldom fatal.

Alaskan mushrooms that contain these toxins are numerous and include:

•Species of gilled mushrooms in the genus *Agaricus* usually distinguished by a distinctly unpleasant phenol odor

•Several red-pored boletes: *Neoboletus luridiformis* and *Rubroboletus eastwoodiae*

- Several species in the genus *Russula* such as *R. emetica*

- *Paxillus involutus*

- *Verpa bohemica* (for some people)

- *Turbinellus (Gomphus) floccosus*

- *Laetiporus conifericola* if uncooked

- *Ramaria formosa* and relatives

Symptoms usually appear within an hour but can take up to four hours to show up. They include mild to acute nausea, vomiting, diarrhea and abdominal cramps. Symptoms become less intense after the body gets rid of the problem-causing amino acids. If symptoms become severe, medical treatment and hospitalization are necessary to maintain fluid and electrolyte balance. Fortunately, only in rare cases, death can occur from heart failure without fluid and electrolyte replacement. If you suspect mushroom poisoning, seek medical help immediately. Once again, if possible, take uncooked specimens with you.

Raw, under cooked or eating large quantities of some mushrooms, can also cause this poisoning. Some people are more sensitive to the amino acids that cause it. Others are immune. For example, years ago, I shared a meal of Chanterelles with a friend. I was fine with the meal. He was not. His poisoning could have been the result of an individual hypersensitivity or just one "bad" mushroom in the batch. Always carefully examine each specimen before cooking and consuming.

3. MUSCARINE

This toxin occurs in a handful of species. It can cause visual impairment, excessive tears, perspiration and salivation, difficulty breathing, low blood pressure and an irregular heartbeat. In severe cases, fatalities result from respiratory failure. Other symptoms include nausea, vomiting and diarrhea. Symptoms appear within 30 minutes after the mushrooms are eaten and usually go away within 24 hours.

Alaskan mushrooms containing muscarine include:

- Red-pored Boletes

- *Clitocybe dealbata*

- *Mycena pura*

- *Entoloma rhodopolium*

- Several species in the genus *Inocybe*

Muscarine which is harmless in trace amounts, has been found in Boletes, *Hygrocybe, Lactarius* and *Russula* species. It is a trace compound in the Fly Agaric *Amanita muscaria*; the more relevant toxic compound in this species is muscimol.

4. IBOTENIC ACID, MUSCIMOL and similar ISOXAZOLE DERIVA-TIVES

Several poisonous mushrooms of the genus *Amanita*—most notably the Fly Agaric, *A. muscaria* and the Panther, *A. regalis (pantherina)*—contain muscimol and ibotenic acid. Muscimol inhibits the activity of neurons in the brain. Ibotenic acid is a potent neurotoxin and is structurally similar to glutamate that activates the NMDA receptors important for controlling synaptic plasticity and memory function.

These poisons cause delirium, what can be mistaken for inebriation and manic behavior. Some victims report seeing small objects appearing very large. (Think Grace Slicks' "White Rabbit".) Others enjoy intense physical activity under the influence of these poisons. Nausea and vomiting may also occur. By affecting the central nervous system, they cause confusion, visual distortion, a feeling of strength, delusions and convulsions. Drowsiness is also common. Many who eat these mushrooms fall into a deep sleep during which they experience visions.

Symptoms show up half an hour to two hours after ingestion and last up to four hours or more. The best treatment is moral support — to reassure the victim that the effects are temporary. Atropine exacerbates rather than relieves symptoms. As a mycologist told a friend "Take notes"! after the friend had not

7

adequately par boiled *Amanita muscaria* to purge the poisons, bringing on symptoms of muscimol poisoning.

Beware: Another friend of mine lost her beloved golden retriever to *Amanita muscaria*.

5. GYROMITRIN / MONOMETHYLHYDRAZINE (MMH)

Gyromitrin, which is converted to monomethylhydrazine (MMH), and used as a propellant in rocket fuel, is found in some fungi. Symptoms begin seven to ten hours after ingestion and include nausea and vomiting. Victims feel bloated and experience abdominal pain and diarrhea and often a headache. In severe cases, death due to liver damage is possible. There may be cumulative effects.

Several Alaskan *Gyromitra* species: G. esculenta and *G. infula* or false morels, are known to produce these symptoms.

MMH is highly carcinogenic. Members of other genera related to *Gyromitra*, such as *Helvella, Verpa* and *Cudonia*, also contain gyromitrin. There is no antidote for this poisoning; medical treatment is only supportive.

Many people in North America and Europe, continue to eat these mushrooms. Toxins are reduced by thoroughly cooking, or in a process of parboiling by boiling, rinsing, boiling, and rinsing again. But there have been some cases where inhaling the fumes during cooking has sickened the chef! Every mushroom hunter needs to avoid *Gyromitra* and *Helvella*) and other closely related poisonous mushrooms.

There is some evidence *Verpa bohemica* is edible. I debated whether to include it in the first book of this series: *Edible Mushrooms of Alaska*. I have eaten this species, as have many people I know with no problems. But I wonder about it's cumulative effects, which are difficult to determine. If you decide to try it for the first time, eat a little at first to make sure you are not susceptible and be sure they are well cooked.

6. COPRINE

Several mushrooms contain the amino acid coprine, which interacts negatively with alcohol in the human body. Coprine exacerbates the symptoms of alcohol intoxication. One could say these mushrooms are not poisonous and that alcohol is the toxin. Coprine containing mushrooms should not be eaten before, with, or after drinking alcohol. After this fungus is eaten, symptoms begin thirty minutes to two hours later. They include an increased pulse rate, flushing on the upper half of the body, headache, and rapid breathing. Fifteen to thirty minutes later, the victim feels weak and dizzy and usually experiences nausea and vomiting.

Coprine poisoning can continue for several days to a week after eating the mushroom and can reoccur if someone drinks alcohol two or more days after eating the mushrooms.

Alaskan mushrooms reported causing coprine poisoning include *Coprinopsis atramentarius* and *Clitocybe clavipes*.

7. PSILOCYBIN / PSILOCIN

The alkaloids Psilocybin and psilocin interact with the brain, binding to receptors for the neurotransmitter serotonin and also affecting nerve transmission. Fifteen to sixty minutes after ingestion, the victim experiences anxiety, giddiness, hallucinations, the perception of motion by stationary objects, strange time and distance perception and euphoria. As time goes on, they can experience bouts of uncontrolled laughter. Several hours later, victims typically fall asleep and experience intense and colorful dreams. Some research has shown a feeling of euphoria can continue for over a year after ingestion of *Psilocybe*. For an excellent read on this check out *How to Change Your Mind* by Michael Pollan. Mushrooms reported to cause psilocybin-psilocin poisoning include species of *Gymnopilus, Panaeolus, Pluteus* (not our common species, *Pluteus cervinus*) and *Psilocybe*.

Rules to prevent mushroom poisoning:

• Never eat a wild mushroom without knowing for sure what it is, or a mushroom expert confirms it is edible. When in doubt, throw it out!

• Never eat a mushroom raw except for a few jellies and cups that are too watery to cook, otherwise cook your mushrooms.

• Don't collect mushrooms from polluted areas such as mines, heavily traveled roads and areas sprayed with herbicides, insecticides or fungicides.

• If you do eat wild mushrooms, not widely known to be safe, save a few uncooked specimens for identification should you become ill.

There is no hard and fast rule that can tell you if a mushroom is poisonous or edible. Know the mushrooms you choose to eat. Make sure you know the ones that can kill you. These rules cannot be over stressed.

Over and above their use in the kitchen, the diversity and beauty of Alaska's many fungal species makes getting to know them a fun and joyful experience. I hope this book adds to your repertoire of tools to help you along your path on the fascinating journey to understanding Alaskan fungi.

Acknowledgements

This series of mushroom books could not have fruited without the love and support of my partner in the wilderness and other life explorations, Terry Jacobson. Special thanks also are given to my fellow fungal foraging photographer friends: Michele Cornelius and Gene Cornelius for editing help and suggestions. Also, thanks to John Denk, Jason Hollinger creator of *Mushroom Observer. org*, Michael Beug author of *Ascomycete Fungi of North America: A Mushroom Reference Guide* and Steve Trudell author of *Mushrooms of the Pacific Northwest* for their excellent advice and guidance. Last but not least, thanks to the photographers who allowed me to use their work. Most are used under the Creative Commons license at Wikimedia. When a photographic credit is not given in the comment segment of the description, the photo is my own.

Be sure to purchase from these Alaskan bookstores: Parnassus in Ketchikan, Sing Lee Alley in Petersburg, Old Harbor Books in Sitka, Hearthside Books and Rainy Retreat Books in Juneau, The Bookstore in Haines, Skaguay News Depot, The Homer Bookstore and Fireside Books in Palmer.

Gilled Mushrooms with White Spores

Amanita augusta   **Western Yellow Veil**

Cap: Brownish, ochraceous-brown to buff-brown to yellow with yellowish-gray patches, convex, expanding to flat-convex with incurved margin becoming decurved, 3-16 cm across **Gills:** White to yellow-white, close, adnexed to free, tinged yellowish near cap margin **Spore Print:** White **Stalk:** Loose, cream yellow colored ring on upper stalk, stuffed, tapering to enlarged, powdery, friable universal veil forms a scaly volva or scaly zones and/or yellow to grayish-yellow powdery scales at base of stem, volva easily deteriorates **Veil:** Universal veil with yellowish gray or yellow warts or scales arranged concentrically on basal bulb, becoming grayish-yellow, partial veil membranous, cream colored, forming a fragile superior, skirt-like ring with a yellowish margin **Flesh:** White to pale yellowish, soft **Habitat:** On ground in mixed forests, solitary or in small groups **Edibility:** Not known to be edible, avoid. **Comments:** *A. aspera* and *A. franchetii* are misapplied names. *A. augusta* can be confused with browner forms of *A. pantherina* (and probably *A. regalis*) but ring and warts on cap are not white and volva differs. *A. pantherina* may not be in Alaska but should be watched for none-the-less. The Western Yellow Veil is common, especially in Southeast Alaska. The yellow veil, not cap color, is its most reliable characteristic.

Amanita constricta   Constricted Amanita

Cap: White to various shades of dark brown with radially furrowed margin, oval becoming convex to plane or slightly umbonate, often with inconspicuous, radial, dark streaks, viscid when moist, cap top bald or covered with a patch of membranous universal veil tissue, somewhat fibrillose, 4-13 cm across **Gills:** White or grayish, close, adnate to adnexed or free **Spore Print:** White **Stalk:** Often with grayish scales, equal or tapers upward, lower volva constricted with top flaring out, inner surface often tan or gray, often bruises reddish when wet, may disintegrate when old **Veil:** Pale gray to charcoal, universal but no partial veil **Flesh:** White to grayish, fragile, thin **Habitat:** On ground under or near conifers **Edibility:** It is unknown if all are edible, but included here since it is best to avoid all members of this genus **Comments:** Uncommon in Alaska. The volva on *A. vaginata* (widespread in Alaska) is attached only at the stem bottom while in the *A. constricta* group, the volva is firmly attached partway up the stem flaring open at the top.

Amanita muscaria   Fly Agaric

Cap: Blood-red, scarlet-red or orange-red often fading to orange, yellow-orange or paler with pyramid-like, white patches, spherical becoming convex then flat to somewhat depressed, warts flattened with age, wearing away or washed off by rain, cap viscid when moist, margin usually somewhat striate, 5-40 cm broad **Gills:** Whitish, free or slightly attached **Spore Print:** White **Stalk:** Ringed with bulbous base **Veil:** Universal veil white **Flesh:** White, firm when young, soft with age **Habitat:** On ground under pine, Spruce and Birch **Edibility:** Poisonous, causing delirium, raving and perfuse sweating; edible if meticulously par boiled, but any more on the process is beyond the scope of this book **Comments:** Named from its use when mixed with milk to stupefy houseflies. *A. muscaria* var. *formosa* is similar but has a yellowish cap with pinkish-buff patches. Very common throughout Alaska and the Yukon.

Amanita regalis   Panther Cap

Cap: Brownish with white patches that may wash off in rain, round to convex, becoming plane to slightly depressed, 5-25 cm broad **Gills:** Whitish turning pallid, adnate to adnexed or free, close **Spore Print:** White **Stalk:** Whitish enlarging toward rounded basal bulb **Veil:** White, membranous, forming a skirt on middle or upper stalk, margin toothed or ragged **Flesh:** White, firm **Habitat:** On ground under conifers **Edibility:** Poisonous, contains muscarine in higher amounts than *A. muscaria* **Comments:** Varieties range from white, yellow or brownish, all spotted like a panther. Differs from *A. augusta* by the color of the patches. Dr. Gary Laursen names *Amanita muscaria* var *regalis* as the Panther Cap. It is more common in the Interior.

Amanita porphyria — Gray-veil Amanita

Cap: Grayish-brown with slight purple tinge, convex, becoming broadly convex, sticky when young or wet, smooth, usually with scattered grayish or sometimes whitish warts, these sometimes merging to form a patch or often wearing off or washing away in the rain, slightly viscid when moist, margin not striate or only faintly so, 3-12 cm broad **Gills:** Creamy white, sometimes graying or in age bruising grayish, free or attached, close, numerous, short sub-gills **Spore Print:** White **Stalk:** Whitish with small grayish fibers and gray-brown patches, gray veil, grayish volva sometimes leaving fragments on lower stem **Veil:** Ashy gray, thin, membranous, collapsing against stem or partial veil membranous, forms a superior to middle, skirt-like ring that can collapse or disappear with age, ring gray to grayish yellow **Flesh:** Whitish, thin, odor often turnip-like when older **Habitat:** Solitary or in groups of several, under conifers and mixed woods **Edibility:** Not known to cause poisonings but contains the same toxins as *A. muscaria* and should not be eaten **Comments:** The best distinguishing characteristic is the stem surface which has a gray chevron pattern and the grey veil. Some years this species can be quite common, at least in Southeast Alaska. Also found in the Yukon.

Hygrophoropsis aurantiaca   **False Chanterelle**

Cap: Dark orange, yellow-orange, sometimes appearing banded, convex to nearly plane at maturity, disc often depressed, incurved margin, becoming decurved, dry, finely tomentose, 2.5-7 cm broad **Gills:** Orange, usually brighter than cap, descending, narrow, close, repeatedly forked **Spore Print:** White to cream **Stalk:** Orange-brown to yellowish, equal to enlarged at base, dry **Flesh:** Pallid to pale orange, thin **Habitat:** On ground or on decayed coniferous wood and logs **Edibility:** To be avoided. Some people eat this species but it is not all that flavorful and lacks texture. Some sources list it as mildly poisonous. **Comments:** Thinner and lighter than its alleged look-a-like: *Cantharellus formosus.* Also in the Yukon. A poisonous unrelated species is *Turbinellus floccosus,* the Scaly Chanterelle. It is vase-shaped with a reddish to orange-buff scaly cap and resembles a Chanterelle. It can cause nausea, vomiting, and diarrhea 8-14 hours after ingestion and can harm the liver.

Hygrocybe conica   **Witch's Hat**

Cap: Yellow, orange or reddish to scarlet orange, often with olive to greenish tints, to black, sometimes convex, sharply to broadly conic and remaining so, slimy when fresh, but soon dry or tacky; smooth or finely hairy in age, all parts bruise black, some older specimens are completely black, 2-7 cm broad **Gills:** Whitish becoming yellowish-orange or olive orange, nearly free, close, bruising black **Spore Print:** White **Stalk:** Colored like cap, equal, moist but not slimy, fragile, splitting, hollow, often twisted, bruising black **Flesh:** Colored like cap, thin, blackening, odor not distinctive **Habitat:** Singly or in groups, saprophytic under hardwoods and conifers and in grass **Edibility:** Taste not distinctive; some reports indicate it is edible, may be slightly hallucinogenic, not recommended **Comments:** Widespread in Alaska and the Yukon but not in great numbers. Formerly known as *Hygrophorus conicus.* It is the most common and widely distributed species in the cluster of species that forms the witch's hat complex.

Lactarius repraesentaneus   Yellow Bearded Milk Cap

Cap: Straw-yellow to orange-yellow, sticky surface, bruising purplish, convex with incurved margin, bearded margin when young, becoming flat to shallowly depressed **Gills:** Cream to ochre, adnate to slightly decurrent, attached, close to crowded **Spore Print:** Yellowish **Stalk:** White to yellow-orange, short, hollow, spotted, slimy when fresh **Latex:** Abundant, white to cream, becoming violet **Flesh:** White, staining lilac to violet **Habitat:** On ground under Spruce and in mixed Spruce-hardwood forests. **Edibility:** Probably poisonous **Comments:** Common throughout Alaska.

Lactarius rufus   Red-hot Milky

Cap: Red to reddish-brown, concentric zones, convex becoming plane or depressed, with tiny knob in center and incurved margin, becoming flat to vase-shaped, 3-13 cm across **Gills:** Pale, tinged cap color, attached or slightly decurrent, sometimes forked **Spore Print:** Whitish to pale yellow **Stalk:** Base whitish, otherwise same as cap or paler **Latex:** White, unchanging **Flesh:** Dingy reddish to purplish, thin, rather soft **Habitat:** Single or in groups, on ground under Spruce, mixed hardwood-conifer forests and sphagnum bogs **Edibility:** Peppery acrid to bland, can cause gastric disturbance **Comments:** Widespread in Alaska and the Yukon.

Lactarius scrobiculatus   Pitted Milk Cap

Cap: Yellow-orange, scaly with inrolled, hairy margin, broadly convex with depressed disc, becoming flatter and funnel-shaped, 7-20 cm broad **Gills:** White to yellowish **Spore Print:** White to bright creamy yellow **Stalk:** Tawny with glazed yellow-brown spots, pitted, downy, sometimes tapering to a root-like base, with brighter colored depressed spots, hollow **Latex:**

White, plentiful, quickly changing to sulfur-yellow **Flesh:** White, rigid, odor fruity, taste burning-acrid or mild or slightly peppery **Habitat:** Single or in groups under conifers, especially pines **Edibility:** Poisonous, do not eat any *Lactarius* with white latex that turns yellow **Comments:** Found at least in Southeast and the Interior. Recognized by pale yellow to dark ocher color, with shallow pits on stem and white milk that quickly turns yellow and stains exposed tissues yellowish.

Lactarius torminosus — Woolly Milky

Cap: Pinkish with white, bearded, inrolled margin, woolly, convex then slightly depressed, with slightly darker concentric circles, 5-15 cm broad **Gills:** Pink to whitish, becoming tan, crowded **Spore Print:** Pale yellowish-cream **Stalk:** Pink or paler than cap, dry, smooth to fuzzy, sometimes spotted, ages to smooth and hollow **Latex:** White or pale cream, very acrid and does not change color **Flesh:** White to pink-tinged, brittle **Habitat:** Single or in groups on ground, usually under Birch **Edibility:** Not recommended; taste burning-peppery. It is added to coffee in Norway. If eaten without very careful preparation, this mushroom can cause stomach upsets. Some authorities suggest that the Woolly Milky is edible after it has been salted and pickled, but many more treat it as poisonous. **Comments:** Widespread. In Latin, *torminosus* means "cause of colic".

Lactarius uvidus   Violet-latex Milk Cap

Cap: Lilac-drab, convex to flat, finally somewhat sunken, margin incurved at first, smooth, sticky, becoming dry **Gills:** White when young, in age pale tan, beginning to run down stem, close **Spore Print:** Pale yellow **Stalk:** Off-white, bruising or discoloring brownish at base, equal, smooth **Latex:** White, stains gills and flesh purplish **Flesh:** Whitish, firm, becoming purplish when sliced **Habitat:** Under conifers **Edibility:** Poisonous, mild or somewhat bitter **Comments:** A poorly understood species complex, avoid all purple staining Milk Caps.

Russula emetica   The Sickener

Cap: Reddish, slimy, fleshy, smooth, convex to flattened or slightly depressed, viscid when wet, shiny, peel separates easily, margin strongly striated, 6-9 cm across **Gills:** Off-white, attached, slightly adnexed to free, close, broad, narrow near stem **Spore Print:** White to yellowish white **Stalk:** Off-white to tinged red, nearly equal, smooth, spongy, stuffed **Flesh:** White, brittle, red under peel **Habitat:** Single or in scattered groups usually in moss, on ground or on very rotten wood **Edibility:** Poisonous, symptoms gastrointestinal: nausea, vomiting, diarrhea and abdominal cramps and usually begin half an hour to three hours after ingestion **Comments:** Common and widespread in Alaska and the Yukon.

Russula foetens   Fetid Russula

Cap: Yellowish to dingy brown, smooth, viscid, margin coarsely striated, 5-15 cm across **Gills:** Whitish becoming yellowish with age, dingy where bruised, adnexed, close, exuding water drops when young **Spore Print:** White **Stalk:** White to dingy brown with age, equal, smooth, stuffed, becoming hollow and chambered in age **Flesh:** White to yellowish under peel, thin, fragile, strong unpleasant odor resembling that of bitter almonds, then fetid **Habitat:** Singly or in groups on ground in mixed woods **Edibility:** If eaten raw causes vomiting; if cooked may cause poisoning for some people **Comments:** In the *R. fragrantissima group*. Another poisonous *Russula* is *R. densiflora* and it is boring and maybe poisonous. It stains red and then black.

Ampulloclitocybc clavipes   Fat-footed Gymnopus

Cap: Buff to gray-brown with olivaceous tint, paling toward margin, flattened, convex with slight umbo at first, later depressed, moist, smooth, with matted hairs and scuffy disc, 2-8 cm broad **Gills:** White to pale creamy yellow, deeply descending stalk, distantly narrow to broad **Spore Print:** White **Stalk:** Whitish to ash, greatly enlarged, spongy base covered in silky fibers **Flesh:** White, thick, spongy, rather brittle when dry, often fragrant, fruity like grapes **Habitat:** On ground under conifers **Edibility:** With caution; some individuals eating this species with alcohol have experienced coprine poisoning similar to that caused by eating *Coprinopsis atramentaria* with alcohol: headache, hot flashes, internal disturbances, rash **Comments:** There are many more or less similar species. Formerly known as *Clitocybe clavipes*.

Clitocybe rivulosa — Sweating Mushroom

Cap: Dull white, smooth, small, convex at first with margin incurved and narrowly inrolled, expanding to flat with depressed disc, margin arched when old, 2-4 cm broad **Gills:** Whitish or cream, slightly descending stalk, attached, nearly distant, narrow to broad **Spore Print:** White **Stalk:** White, smooth, fibrous, tough **Flesh:** Whitish, thin, except for center of cap, faint smell **Habitat:** Scattered to numerous or in rings on ground in grass and open woods **Edibility:** Poisonous and potentially fatal to children due to muscarine which causes profuse sweating, salivation, diarrhea, etc; toxic look a-like of the Fairy-ring Mushroom **Comments:** Formerly known as *Clitocybe dealbata*. "Dealbata" means bleached.

Clitocybe dilatata   **Crowded White Clitocybe**

Cap: White, chalky-white sometimes with buffy areas, large, clustered, overlapping, convex to flat or often somewhat misshapen, margin incurved, often becoming wavy, smooth, when old broadly and shallowly depressed, usually deformed from adjacent caps, 1.5-15 cm across **Gills:** Whitish to buff, attached to slightly descending stalk **Spore Print:** White **Stalk:** White, dry, fibrous **Flesh:** White to grayish, firm, thick on disc **Habitat:** Densely clustered in sandy or gravelly soil along roads and trails **Edibility:** Poisonous, contains muscarine. **Comments:** Formerly known as *Clitocybe connata* but could actually be *Leucocybe connata*.

Connopus acervatus   **Clustered Collybia**

Cap: Reddish-brown fading to brown or buff, watery, margin incurved, paler, fades to white, upturned when mature, broadly convex with age, glabrous, clustered, 1-5 cm broad **Gills:** Whitish to pinkish, adnate to free, attached or nearly free, close or crowded **Spore Print:** White **Stalk:** Two-toned, reddish-brown, flattened, dry, smooth, hollow, fine whitish hairs over lower half or at base **Flesh:** Pinkish-white, thin, flexible, odor not distinctive **Habitat:** Clustered to tufted on coniferous logs, base of Cottonwood and Spruce and on decayed wood **Edibility:** Has a bitter taste when cooked, poisonous to some people. **Comments:** Common in Southeast Alaska.. Also in the Yukon. Formerly known as *Collybia acervata* and *Gymnopus acervatus*.

Pleurocybella porrigens   Angel Wings

Cap: White, broad, thin-fleshed, laterally attached, margin inrolled and slightly striate, later flattening, watery **Gills:** White, descending to stub-like, close, narrow, linear, sometimes forking near base **Spore Print:** White **Stalk:** Stalkless **Flesh:** White, thin, fragile **Habitat:** In overlapping shelf-like clusters on coniferous wood, especially hemlock **Edibility:** Although thin-fleshed, angel wings is a fairly popular edible mushroom. However, it has been responsible for several deaths (under unusual circumstances). Eating it, especially in large amounts, is not recommended until more is known. **Comments:** Formerly known as *Pleurotus porrigens* and *Pleurotellus porrigens*. Also found in the Yukon.

Cystoderma amianthinum   Pungent Cystoderma

Cap: Pale reddish-brown to yellow-brown or yellowish, conical to convex to nearly flat, usually wrinkled in radial patterns, dry, granular, 2-5 cm across **Gills:** Whitish becoming pale yellowish, attached, crowded, narrow **Spore Print:** White **Stalk:** Off-white above ring, ochre-buff below **Veil:** Fragile, ring small on stem or often evanescent **Flesh:** Disagreeable, pungent, like freshly husked corn. **Habitat:** In moss, humus or coniferous needles **Edibility:** Avoid, not well studied in Alaska and can be confused with poisonous species. **Comments:** Very common worldwide.

Cystoderma fallax   Common Conifer Cystoderma

Cap: Rusty-orange to cinnamon to tawny-ochre, convex to flat, umbonate, with mealy granules which are erect at first but flattened and more powdery in age, can be washed off by rain, margin often hung with veil remnants, 2-5 cm across **Gills:** Whitish, attached, close, narrow, granular **Spore Print:** White **Stalk:** Off-white and smooth above prominent ring, can be slightly bulbous **Veil:** Reddish-brown, granular, persistent annulus **Flesh:** Whitish or tinged cap color **Habitat:** On moss and in leaf litter **Edibility:** Unknown, to be avoided **Comments:** Also known as *C. carcharias* var. *fallax* and is found in the Yukon too. Rustier than *C. amianthinum* which lacks a well-formed ring.

Lepiota magnispora   Yellowfoot Dapperling

Cap: Buff-yellow to brownish scales shading to smooth, disc brown, egg-shaped then bell-shaped to convex to nearly plane with low umbo, dry, margin ragged with veil filaments **Gills:**

24

White to cream with age, free, close, narrow **Spore Print:** White **Stalk:** Yellowish-buff with shaggy scales, veil with woolly patches leaving fragments on cap margin **Veil:** Partial, does not form a well developed ring **Flesh:** White to yellowish, odor not distinctive **Habitat:** Scattered to grouped under hardwoods and conifers **Edibility:** Unknown but should be avoided. Some small *Lepiota* species are known to contain the same toxins as *Amanita phalloides*, the Death Cap **Comments:** *Lepiota* species are uncommon in Alaska and documented primarily in the Interior. Formerly known as *L. ventriosospora*.

Lepista irina   Woolly Lepista

Cap: Off-white to dingy buff, but can be a bit pinkish, sometimes pitted or with watery spots and cottony margin at first, obtuse expanding to flat or nearly so, margin inrolled becoming horizontal to lobed or wavy, rounded at first, often umbonate in expanded caps, occasionally grooved from pressure against gills, 3-13 cm across **Gills:** Whitish to buff to pale pink, adnate or broadly adnate to subdecurrent, crowded, narrow to moderately broad **Spore Print:** Pale cream or pale pinkish buff. This species could also be placed in the pink spored section. **Stalk:** White, becoming grayish yellowish-brown, solid, equal to club-shaped, sometimes rather bulbous, fibrillose to slightly scabrous, sometimes scaly from torn cuticle, base with numerous mycelium strands incorporating surrounding needles and duff **Veil:** Lacking **Flesh:** Sharply pungent or fragrant but also almost odorless **Habitat:** Gregarious to in more or less in tufts, under Spruce **Edibility:** This was considered choice like its relative *L. nuda* but there have been gastrointestinal poisonings reported. Other reports are that it is poisonous to some. Should be cooked well if you decide to take a chance. **Comments:** Uncommon. Also in the Yukon.

Tricholoma equestre   Man on Horseback

Cap: Yellow with fine reddish-brown, appressed hairs on crown, viscid, robust, convex, becoming nearly plane with age, 5-13 cm broad **Gills:** Bright yellow, close, notched, broad **Spore Print:** White **Stalk:** Pale yellow to white or white with yellow spots, equal to enlarged at base **Flesh:** Whitish or tinged yellow **Habitat:** Under deciduous trees such as Aspen and Birch and also conifers . Has a coconut odor. **Edibility:** Uncertain. It has been listed as edible and excellent but some people are adversely affected by it. Sources in Europe say not recommended: there are reports of poisoning, even death and the species is not well understood. **Comments:** Formerly known as *T. flavovirens.* Also in the Yukon.

Tricholoma myomyces   Earth-colored Tricholoma

Cap: Dark gray to blackish over pallid background, convex to plano-convex, disk can be slightly elevated, incurved margin wavy with fibrils, becoming decurved, 1.5-4.5 cm broad **Gills:** Pale-gray, pallid with age, abruptly adnexed to adnate **Spore Print:** White **Stalk:** Pallid when young, light-gray in age **Veil:** Partial veil fibrillose, evanescent, leaving remnants high on stalk **Flesh:** Gray, thin, odor mild, taste like cucumber **Habitat:** Scattered to gregarious under conifers **Edibility:** Avoid, not enough is known about this species, may contain gastrointestinal irritants **Comments:** Found in Southeast Alaska and the Interior. Formerly known as *T. terreum*. *T. pardinum* also has a gray, scaly cap, is larger and toxic and known from British Columbia, so may be in Alaska.

Tricholoma platyphyllum   Northwest Stinker

Cap: White to creamy, convex to slightly depressed, smooth, more or less bald, margin entire, 3-5 cm across **Gills:** White, very broad and widely spaced, distended **Spore Print:** White **Stalk:** Pure white, smooth, bald, widening downwards to swollen base **Veil:** Absent **Flesh:** Rather thick with obnoxious coal tar odor **Habitat:** Under conifers in humus **Edibility:** Poisonous **Comments:** Do not confuse its name with that of *Megacollybia platyphylla.*

Tricholoma sejunctum   Separating Trich

Cap: Yellowish-green to grayish-brown towards disc, radially streaked, moist, sticky to dry, knobbed, 5-7.5 cm broad **Gills:** Whitish, notched, often yellow near the margin of the cap or sometimes overall, close **Spore Print:** White **Stalk:** Whitish, flushing yellowish, dry, silky-fibrillose **Flesh:** White, in older specimens yellowing below cap cuticle **Habitat:** In deciduous and coniferous woods **Edibility:** Bitter and mealy, nauseating, poisonous at worst, insipid at best **Comments:** Throughout Alaska

Tricholomopsis decora   Decorated Mop

Cap: Deep golden with blackish fibrous scales on disc, convex at first becoming centrally depressed, 6-17 cm broad **Gills:** Yellow, narrow, attached, crowded **Spore Print:** White **Stalk:** Sulfur to pale yellow, minutely scaly, occasionally bent or off-center, equal, solid to hollow when fresh with scattered grayish fibrils toward the base and the apex **Flesh:** Deep yellow, thin, odor almost none to not distinctive, taste mild to bitterish **Habitat:** On conifer logs or humus **Edibility:** Unknown, avoid. **Comments:** More common in Southeast Alaska.

Megacollybia platyphylla   **Broad-gill**

Cap: Brownish-gray appearing streaked with radially appressed fibers, disk sometimes darker and tomentose, bell-shaped becoming convex to flat, dry, margin incurved then decurved, wavy to indented, 6-10 cm broad **Gills:** White, cream to pale gray, adnexed to notched, attached, broad **Spore Print:** White **Stalk:** White, lower part streaked with brown fibrils, more or less equal, thick white rhizomorphs at occasionally enlarged base **Flesh:** White, firm, thin at margin, coal tar odor **Habitat:** On or near coniferous and deciduous logs **Edibility:** Questionable, bad reactions have occurred **Comments:** Formerly known as *Tricholomopsis platyphylla*.

Gilled Mushrooms with Pink Spores

Nolanea strictior   Strict Nolanea

Cap: Bell-shaped to convex to upturned, margin down curved, then flat to uplifted; hygrophanous, two-colored, dark brown to dark gray brown on cap top, medium brown elsewhere, then faded brownish orange everywhere; dull, bald, 2-6 cm across **Gills:** Almost free, close, narrow to moderately broad, pallid to whitish when young, edges colored as faces; edges smooth then eroded **Spore Print:** Salmon-pink or pinkish-cinnamon **Stalk:** Silky white; when old becoming brownish orange; widening downward, round in cross-section, hollow; basal mycelium abundant **Flesh:** Thin and fragile **Habitat:** Single to scattered in mossy humus or in Sphagnum moss **Edibility:** Avoid **Comments:** Common, at least in Southeast Alaska.

Entoloma rhodopolium   Rosy Entoloma

Cap: Dark gray to yellowish-buff, convex with a slight umbo then expanded and often depressed, 3-7 cm broad **Gills:** Whitish then flesh-pink, adnate or notched, fairly close to rather well-spaced, indistinctly wavy, close or subdistant, narrow or narrow to moderately broad **Spore Print:** Pink **Stalk:** White to silky grayish **Veil:** Absent **Flesh:** White, but when moist and water-soaked, colored as cap, when faded, pallid except directly beneath the cap surface, thin, firm, smells mealy **Habitat:** Single, scattered or in groups or clusters on ground and leaf litter in woods, mainly under hardwoods especially *Alnus rubra* (red alder) **Edibility:** Poisonous causing gastric upset and abdominal cramps that may send you to the hospital **Comments:** Southeast Alaska where uncommon. *Nolaneas* are slender and do not have the *Tricholoma*-like stature of the *E. rhodopolium* group.

Gilled Mushrooms with Dark Spores

Agaricus moelleri   Scaly Flat-top

Cap: Whitish background with flattened inky-grayish-brown or brown fibrils especially at cap top, dry, 5-25 cm across **Gills:** Close, free, pallid then gray or light pink, then reddish-chocolate brown and then chocolate brown **Spore Print:** Chocolate-brown **Stalk:** White, discoloring to reddish brown or dingy brown, equal to enlarged at base, without scales **Veil:** Membranous, white, thick and felt-like or rubbery, can split at margin **Flesh:** White, thick, unchanging or stains slightly yellow, odor phenolic **Habitat:** Single or clustered under conifers **Edibility:** Poisonous, causing vomiting and diarrhea, has an unpleasant metallic taste **Comments:** What is great about *Agaricus* species? The edible ones smell good, while the inedible ones do not. If you do eat a poisonous one, the result is short-term gastrointestinal distress. Formerly known as *A. meleagris* and *A. praeclaresquamosus*.

Coprinopsis atramentaria   Alcohol Inky

Cap: Gray to gray brown, ovoid then broadly conical when expanded, margin first with irregular puckers, then splitting, smooth or silky with minute veil remnants especially near disk, 3-7 cm tall **Gills:** White, then lavender gray, then inky black and soon deliquescing, free, crowded **Spore Print:** Black **Stalk:** Whitish, dry, silky-fibrous, hollow **Veil:** White, partial, leaving ring zone near base **Flesh:** Faint odor **Habitat:** In clusters on ground near rotting wood or in grassy areas and gardens **Edibility:** Edible but poisonous if eaten before, during, or after drinking alcohol (coprine poisoning). Symptoms occur 5-10 minutes after an Inky is eaten and include tingling in arms and legs, nausea, vomiting, metallic taste in mouth, headache, sweating, confusion, low blood pressure, and collapse. Ink made from the deliquesced caps by boiling with a little water and cloves **Comments:** Similar species *C. micaceus* has a tan to yellow brown cap, thinner stem and is less fleshy with gills pallid soon becoming gray or brownish then black, striate at least halfway to center. Both species formerly placed in *Coprinus* genus.

Panaeolus foenisecii　　　Haymakers Mushroom

Cap: Chestnut brown to cinnamon brown when moist, conical to bell-shaped expanding to convex with umbo to nearly flat, smooth to faintly wrinkled, margin often with dark band, 1.5-3 cm broad **Gills:** Brown to deep brown in age, edges lighter, mottled at maturity, adnate to adnexed, fairly close **Spore Print:** Deep or purple brown **Stalk:** White to dingy-brown, equal to tapering downward, darker at base **Veil:** Absent **Flesh:** Fragile, thin **Habitat:** Lawns and grassy areas **Edibility:** Harmless in small amounts, may or may not contain traces of psilocybin **Comments:** Formerly known as *Panaeolina foenisecii.* This is a very common and widely distributed little brown mushroom (LGB) often found on lawns. Studies show is contains serotonin. It has been listed as psychoactive; but the mushroom does not produce hallucinogenic effects.

Paxillus involutus　　　Poison Pax

Cap: Brownish to dingy yellowish-brown, convex, becoming broadly convex, usually broadly depressed, dry to slimy with inrolled striate margin then decurved, 5-15 cm broad **Gills:** Yellowish, descending, crowded to close, easily pealed from cap, sometimes forming rudimentary pores near stalk **Spore Print:** Clay-brown **Stalk:** Yellowish-brown, bruising brown, stout, separable from cap, equal to tapered at base **Flesh:** Buff-brown, thick, slowly darkening when cut, odor mild **Habitat:** In mixed woods, waste places and greenhouses **Edibility:** May cause kidney failure and Immune Hemolytic Anemia which appears suddenly after years of eating. Traditionally eaten in Europe. **Comments:** Common in Alaska and the Yukon.

Cortinarius armillatus  Bracelet Cort

Cap: Orange-brown to reddish brown with radially flattened hairs, margin with rusty veil pieces adhering, 5-12 cm broad **Gills:** Cinnamon to rusty brown in age, adnate, subdistant, broad **Spore Print:** Rusty brown **Stalk:** Dull brown, enlarging toward base with several rusty red to orange concentric bracelet-like zones of universal veil tissue **Cortina:** White and copious, often leaving hairs on upper stem **Veil:** Reddish, fibrillose **Flesh:** Thick, pallid or brownish, odor usually slightly radish-like **Habitat:** Scattered to gregarious in forest humus, can be associated with Birch **Edibility:** Probably poisonous **Comments:** One of our most beautiful mushrooms. Species name means "having a bracelet".

Cortinarius gentilis
Deadly Cort

Cap: Tawny to ochra to deep orange-brown or rusty-yellow, finely hairy, in age fading, conic or bell-shaped at first, expanding somewhat when old but usually retaining an umbo, not viscid, 1-5 cm wide **Gills:** Ochre-yellow, cinnamon-brown to brown, sometimes with grayish to violet tints, adnexed or sinuate, some close to widely spaced **Spore Print:** Rusty-brown **Stalk:** Cinnamon to light yellow at first but soon mainly brownish orange to brown, with irregular bands and patches that are remnants of the yellow veil, more or less equal or narrowing towards base, dry **Veil:** Yellow to pale yellow universal veil, soon disappearing **Flesh:** Yellowish to yellow-brown, thin, odor radish-like **Habitat:** In moss or duff under conifers **Edibility:** Possibly deadly poisonous, can dissolve liver 3 days to two weeks after being eaten, caused damage to rat kidneys; exact toxicity not well established. **Comments:** Found in Southeast north to the Interior.

Cortinarius ominosus
Red-gilled Yellow Cort

Cap: Yellowish to ochre to olive brown, margin often yellow-cinnamon to ochraceous brown or ochraceous buff, sometimes tinted orange-buff when young, when old tinted or streaked with

35

colors on disc, occasionally the overall coloration tinted with light olive-brown, conic to bell-shaped to rounded becoming convex to flat, slightly umbonate, margin slightly inrolled at first then incurved to down-curved, moist to dry, 2-6 cm across **Gills:** Blood-red, dull red to deep red or purple red becoming brownish to brownish orange when old, adnate to decurrent, adnexed or emarginate, crowded, narrow, hidden by cob webby veil when young, often broader in middle when mature, edges even to wavy **Spore Print:** Rust-brown **Stalk:** Yellowish, pale yellow to dull yellow, colored more or less like cap margin, or sometimes rusty-brown from spores, slender, equal to more or less club-shaped or spindle-shaped, the base with light reddish to dull pinkish tones, becoming olivaceous with age in some specimens, sometimes covered with slight silky ring zone near top **Veil:** Cortina yellowish, evanescent **Flesh:** Yellowish, slight odor of radish **Habitat:** Mixed conifer-deciduous forest **Edibility:** Slightly bitter, suspect, to be avoided **Comments:** Known from southeast to south-central to interior Alaska. Used in the dying of wool. Similar to *C. cinnamomeus*. Misapplied name was *C. semisanguineus*.

Cortinarius traganus   Pungent or Lilac Conifer Cort

Cap: Violet to lilac with rusty patches, margin often with veil remnants, dry, 4-13 cm wide **Gills:** Pale cinnamon or ochre-buff becoming cinnamon, well spaced, adnexed to adnate **Spore Print:** Rusty-brown **Stalk:** Lilac or purplish, base bulbous, finely fibrillose, sometimes with areas of white **Cortina:** Pale lilac, leaving hairs on upper stem **Veil:** Whitish tinged to lilac, inconspicuous ring remaining from thick, cob webby veil **Flesh:** Rusty-cinnamon brown, pungent, disagreeable odor **Habitat:** Single or more commonly in groups on ground in moss under conifers **Edibility:** Too smelly to eat. May be poisonous. **Comments:** Widespread and abundant in Alaska.

Galerina marginata   Deadly Galerina

Cap: Brown fading to yellowish or orange brown, margin translucent striate, viscid, convex to flat with small knob, 2-6 cm broad **Gills:** Yellowish to rusty-brown becoming yellowish-orange to same color as cap, pale brown with age, attached, close, broad, adnexed to-short-decurrent **Spore Print:** Rusty brown **Stalk:** Color lighter but similar to cap, hollow **Veil:** Hairy, leaving thin, superior, white, hairy ring **Flesh:** Reddish, semi-transparent in stalk, brownish red in cap **Habitat:** Scattered to ceaspitose on well decayed wood **Edibility:** Deadly, same toxins as the Death Cap and Destroying Angel: amanitin **Comments:** A variable species and a synonym of *Galerina autumnalis. G. paludosa* can also have a superior white ring, but its stalk is long and thin and it fruits in bogs. Can be mistaken for *Psilocybe cyanescens*. Do not eat any ringed little brown mushroom growing on or near wood.

Galerina paludosa   Bog Galerina

Cap: Yellowish-brown, fading to ochraceous buff or a duller yellow, obtusely conic to convex when young, margin incurved against gills, expanding to bell-shaped or broadly convex to nearly flat, usually with conic umbo; hygrophanous, moist, fibrillose, margin translucent-striate before fading, 1.0-2.5 cm across **Gills:** Light brown to honey-colored, close to subdistant, adnate or decurrent, broad, edges whitish, minutely scalloped **Spore Print:** Rust **Stalk:** Light brown, covered with remnants of universal veil, thin **Veil:** At first veil remnants on cap surface, usually with superior to apical, somewhat membranous, white ring or fibrillose zone **Flesh:** Yellowish, colored more or less like cap, thin, fragile, odor and taste not distinctive **Habitat:** Bogs in Sphagnum moss **Edibility:** Unknown but dangerous to eat any *Galerina* **Comments:** Found uncommonly in Southeast Alaska. Photo by Dimitar Bojantchev.

Hebeloma crustuliniforme   Poison Pie

Cap: Buff with darker crown, or creamy, viscid, convex becoming plano-convex with a broad umbo, inrolled edge, 4-9 cm broad **Gills:** Buff with water drops, adnate or notched, crowded often appearing to slightly overlap one another; pallid when young, becoming watery brown and finally dull brown, base sometimes with white threads of mycelium **Spore Print:** Medium dull brown to yellow-brown **Stalk:** White, equal to enlarged at base, apex covered with fine powdery granules, solid **Veil:** Absent **Flesh:** White, solid, with radish odor **Habitat:** In large groups on ground in forest, often in fairy rings and arcs **Edibility:** Poisonous, taste bitter, causes severe gastrointestinal problems.

Inosperma calamistratum   Green-footed Fiberhead

Cap: Dark brown to coffee-brown, bell-shaped to convex, dry, covered with recurved brown scales, especially at top of cap, not radially splitting in age, 1-4 cm broad **Gills:** Brown to rust, attached

Spore Print: Light to dark brown **Stalk:** Like cap, firm, covered with incurved scales, blue-green to olive-green base **Flesh:** White, becoming reddish, thin, with fishy odor **Habitat:** Solitary, scattered or in small groups on ground in mixed woods **Edibility:** Unknown, like many *Inocybes* may contain muscarine and psilocybin may also be present. A poisoning case confirms that it is quite toxic **Comments:** Found in Southeast Alaska and less commonly in interior Alaska. The species name means "curled". The blue green stalk color is not due to psilocybin. Former name *Inocybe calamistrata*.

Inocybe geophylla   **White Fiberhead**

Cap: White to lilac, spotted brown in age, dry with white veil, conic to bell-shaped with umbo to nearly plane in age, margin may split in dry weather, covered with flattened hairs, 1.5-3 cm across **Gills:** White to grayish white to clay colored in age, almost free, sinuate, well-separated, broad **Spore Print:** Dull clay-brown **Stalk:** White to grayish-white, long, thin, equal, or with indistinct knob at base **Veil:** Hairy, superior, soon disappearing **Flesh:** White, disagreeable spermatic odor **Habitat:** Scattered to gregarious under hardwoods and conifers **Edibility:** Poisonous, contains muscarine **Comments:** Found in Spruce-Hemlock forests. Relatively small for an *Inocybe*. Also in the Yukon.

Inocybe lacera   **Torn Fiberhead**

Cap: Brown sometimes olive-tinged at faintly striated margin, dry, fibrous, becoming scaly, convex with slight umbo, sometimes splitting from the margin inward, 1-3 cm broad **Gills:** White at first, soon clay-buff to greenish, attached, close, broad **Spore Print:** Brown **Stalk:** Whitish near apex, brown towards slightly bulbous base **Veil:** Partial cobwebby, evanescent **Flesh:** White, to pale dingy gray , thin, odor mild **Habitat:** Single or in groups on ground especially sandy soils under conifers and hardwoods and along roads **Edibility:** Poisonous **Comments:** Also in the Yukon.

Inocybe fuscodisca Black Nipple Fiberhead

Cap: Brown turning black especially on the margins and prominant umbo; radially flattened fibrils on a pale buff to whitish background; conic becoming bell-shaped and then flat, 1-2.5 cm across **Spore Print:** Brown **Stalk:** Equal, can be bulbous at base; dark brown to olive-brown fibrils over a whitish background below ring zone, pruinose at top, fleeting ring zone **Flesh:** Pale buff **Edibility:** Poisonous **Comments:** Also found in the Yukon. Look also for other poisonous *Inocybes*: *Pseudosperma rimosum*, the Deadly Fiberhead and *Inocybe lilacina*, the Lilac Inocybe.

Inocybes are often confused with edible species because of their similar appearance. Many of them are poisonous. Several species contain muscarine, psilocybin, or psilocin. In Alaska, other poisonous *Inocybes* include: *I. albodisca, I. dulcamera, I. lanuginosa* (also in the Yukon) *I. lilacina, I. napipes, I. nitidiuscula,* and *I. olympiana*. Most likely there are others.

Pseudosperma sororium   **Corn Silk Inocybe**

Cap: Creamy to pale yellowish, sharply conical or bell-shaped when young, expanding in age but retaining prominent umbo, margin sometimes uplifted in age, dry, radially fibrillose to cracked, shading to slightly darker disc, 2.5-6.5 cm broad **Gills:** Becoming yellowish, attached, close to crowded **Spore Print:** Dull brown **Stalk:** White or tinged cap color, equal to slightly enlarged at base **Flesh:** Pallid to buff, thin, strongly pungent, like fresh, green corn **Habitat:** Solitary or scattered mostly under conifers **Edibility:** Poisonous, contains high concentrations of muscarine. **Comments:** Uncommon. Photo by Jason Hollinger.

Phaeolepiota aurea   **Alaska Gold**

Cap: Golden orange-brown with central knob, fine grandular surface which rubs off, margin often fringed, 5-30 cm broad **Gills:** Pale honey to yellow ochre in age, adnate to adnexed **Spore Print:** Yellow ochre to almost orange **Stalk:** Buff overall, hairless above ring, enlarging toward base **Veil:** Partial veil membranous, dark buff, leaving a large superior, upward flaring, persistent ring **Flesh:** Yellowish, firm, thick **Habitat:** Terrestrial, often under or near alder **Edibility:** The cap reported edible but contains toxins such as cyanide that can cause gastric upset so it is not recommended **Comments:** Common in Southeast and South-central Alaska. Has possible anti-tumor properties. Formerly known as *Pholiota aurea* but it is not related to that genus.

Hypholoma fasciculare   **Sulfur Tuft**

Cap: Tawny to yellowish, convex to flat with slight central knob, margin incurved when young, wavy if clustered, disc yellow-orange to tawny-brown, moist, 2-7 cm broad **Gills:** Greenish-yellow becoming sulfur-green, adnate, crowded, narrow, olive-brown from maturing spores **Spore Print:** Purplebrown **Stalk:** Yellowish, sometimes narrow at base, becoming tawny, equal or tapering downward **Veil:** Partial, leaving fibrous zone **Flesh:** Pale yellow, thin, odor not distinctive **Habitat:** Scattered to clustered on logs and stumps **Edibility:** Poisonous, reported to cause liver and kidney damage, gastrointestinal upset, and death. Fortunately it is rarely eaten due to its bitter taste. **Comments:** Formerly known as *Naematoloma fasciculare.*

Pholiota aurivella — Slimy Golden Pholiota

Cap: Yellow-orange to tawny, with large, spot-like scales, slimy in wet weather **Gills:** Whitish to yellow, rusty brown in age **Stalk:** Cream, pale yellow to yellow-brown with dark orange scales. **Veil:** Whitish to pale yellow to light olive-yellow, ring quickly disappears **Spore Print:** Brown **Edibility:** Either edible or will give you a bad tummy ache. I'd leave it alone **Habitat:** In tufts or clusters on dead Aspen in mixed hardwood and White Spruce forests **Comments:** More common in the Interior. Belongs to the *Pholiota aurivella group,* which are difficult to identify in the field. In the Yukon too. Photo by John Carl Jacobs.

Pholiota squarrosa — Scaly Pholiota

Cap: Yellow-brown, straw-yellow to yellow-ochre, covered wlth upturned, triangular brown scales in concentric rings, convex at first, flatten with age but maintain the inrolled margin, 4 to 12 cm across **Gills:** Pale yellow becoming cinnamon as spores mature, often with greenish tinge, crowded, adnate, a cortina-like veil covers the young gills **Spore Print:** Rusty-brown **Stalk:** Yellowish-tawny, upper section distinctly scaly, ring pale and smooth, below ring covered with downward facing scales similar to those on cap **Veil:** Yellowish, partial, leaving ring zone on upper stalk **Flesh:** Very pale yellow, tough, firm, odor earthly, becoming red-brown in stalk base **Habitat:** In clusters at base of coniferous and deciduous trees, sometimes on stumps of felled trees. **Edibility:** Poisonous, causes gastric discomfort within an hour of ingestion. Smells and tastes like a bitter radish **Comments:** In most of Alaska and the Yukon. Common in Southeast Alaska. *Pholiota limonella* and other members of *Pholiota aurivella* group have a viscid to slimy cap.

Pholiota squarrosoides   **Bristly Pholiota**

Cap: Ochre, becoming cinnamon with down-curved tawny, scattered scales near margin, clustered on disc, with a slime layer, obtusely convex with umbo becoming flat, veil remnants on margin, 3-9 cm across **Gills:** Whitish becoming brownish as spores mature, adnate becoming adnexed, crowded, moderately broad **Spore Print:** Brown **Stalk:** Ochre–tawny scales below ring, whitish above **Veil:** Off-white, partial **Flesh:** Whitish, thick, pliant, odorless or with a slight odor of cinnamon rolls. **Habitat:** Singly or clustered on deciduous wood **Edibility:** Long considered edible but known to cause gastric discomfort within an hour after ingestion. **Comments:** Throughout Alaska but less common and paler than the Scaly Pholiota.

Psilocybe cyanescens Wavy-cap or Bluing Psilocybe

Cap: Chestnut brown, fading to yellowish or buff, bruising blue, striate, convex becoming plane with low umbo, tacky, wavy margin, sometimes upturned in age, 2-4 cm across **Gills:** Cinnamon-brown to pale cinnamon brown, becoming dark gray-brown, adnate to ascending **Spore Print:** Purple-brown **Stalk:** Whitish, bruising blue with conspicuous rhizomorphs at base, surface white, smooth to silky **Veil:** Partial, white, fibrillose, forming a superior evanescent, hairy, annular zone **Flesh:** Bruising blue, brittle with age **Habitat:** Coniferous mulch, wood chips and lawns, gregarious, rarely scattered, sometimes forming rings **Edibility:** Hallucinogenic especially raw. Potentially dangerous due to toxic look a-likes: the deadly *Galerina marginata , Conocybe* and *Inocybe* species. **Comments:** Known at least from Southeast Alaska. Photo by Alan Rockefeller.

Stropharia aeruginosa Blue-green Stropharia

Cap: Slimy, green to blue-green, bell-shaped, becoming broadly convex with knob or nearly flat, margin with veil remnants, 2-6 cm across **Gills:** Whitish, lilac-brown, then dingy to purple or gray-brown, attached, close, broad **Spore Print:** Brownish-purple **Stalk:** Whitish to blue covered with small whitish scales, with quickly disappearing ring, cottony-scaly **Veil:** Off-white partial veil, leaving ring that soon disappears on upper stalk **Flesh:** Whitish-blue, no odor **Habitat:** Grassy areas and on wood debris **Edibility:** May be poisonous **Comments:** Found from Juneau to the North Slope. Unlike some *Stropharia* species and other bluish colored mushrooms, has not been shown to contain psilocybin or psilocin. Uncommon.

Mushrooms without Gills

Neoboletus luridiformis   Red-stalked Bolete

Cap: Varying in color from rufous to olive tinge to brown, tending to be yellowish-ochre at margins, staining almost immediately to blue-black, minutely hairy, somewhat tomentose to nearly smooth, dry, margin inrolled becoming expanded, wavy and irregular, 5-15 cm broad **Pores:** Reddish turning blue-black when bruised, small, round **Spore Print:** Olive-brown **Stalk:** Yellowish to orange, obscured by reddish stippling, not reticulate, often bulging in middle and staining blue-black **Flesh:** Greenish yellow to yellow, quickly staining blue when cut **Stalk:** Yellow except reddish at base, solid, rapidly turning blue when exposed **Habitat:** Single or in groups on ground in mixed woods **Edibility:** Edible if cooked for as much as twenty minutes. It is collected in Europe.

Other sources report it is poisonous, causing gastrointestinal distress especially if under cooked. Some people are adversely affected by it and there is a report of one man poisoned by it. **Comments:** Formerly known as *Boletus erythropus.* A related species, *Rubroboletus eastwoodiae* (Satan's Bolete) is toxic, poisonous, causing severe gastrointestinal distress and at least one fatality. It may be or more likely is not in Alaska, but included as one to look out for here as it has been listed in Alaska in the past. It is more likely to be found in California.

Chalciporus piperatus   **Peppery Bolete**

Cap: Rusty brown to vinaceous-brown over a yellowish brown background, convex, becoming broadly convex, nearly plane in age, margin can be wavy at maturity and slightly incurved then decurved, surface sticky when wet, soon dry, smooth to tomentose, especially at margin, 2-7 cm broad **Pores:** Dull yellow-brown to cinnamon brown in age, darkening slightly when bruised, adnate to depressed, attachment usually running a little down the stalk **Spore Print:** Brown **Stalk:** Colored like cap, the base entirely yellow with adhering yellow mycelium **Flesh:** Buff-brown, darkening a little when injured, veil absent **Habitat:** Solitary or scattered under conifers **Edibility:** Caution advised, can cause gastrointestinal discomfort. Peppery taste said to disappear when cooked **Comments:** Yellow at the base is a dead giveaway for ID. Formerly known as *Boletus piperatus.*

Leccinum atrostipitatum   Dark-Stalked Bolete

Cap: Dull to dark orange to tan or brownish, mature cap can have greenish to bluish hues, especially near the margin; dry to slightly viscid, convex, minutely hairy to fibril-streaked, 7–20 cm across **Pores:** Whitish to greenish buff or pale gray when young, becoming dingier with age **Spore Print:** Yellow-brown to olive **Stalk:** Whitish, with many raised, black scabers when young, with age can stain greenish blue around base **Flesh:** White, pink to purple gray to blackish **Habitat:** Fruits on ground in mixed woods, mainly under Birch **Edibility:** Edible, but orange *Leccinum* species have caused poisonings in Alaska. **Comments:** Similar to the next species but they differ in staining reactions (bluish gray with FeSo4 for this species) and microscopically. Similar or the same as *Leccinum versipelle.*

Leccinum aurantiacum   Red–capped Scaber Stalk

Cap: Orange to apricot, to brick-red, rusty red, or reddish brown, becoming dark brown when dry, stains burgundy red at first, then changes to bluish-gray, smooth or slightly downy-fibrillose, convex to broadly convex, to nearly flat when old, dry, dull, appressed-fibrillose when young, margin with thin, conspicuous flaps of sterile tissue when young, often bald when old **Tubes:** White or cream, wine-colored when exposed to air, unchanging or staining olive, brownish or burgundy-brown when cut or bruised, very small round pores, 2-3 per mm **Spore Print:** Ochraceous buff **Stalk:** At first covered with white to buff scabers which turn rusty then orange brown to dark brown and finally blackish brown, at least over the lower portion, occasionally with blue-green or yellowish stains on the lower portion, equal or widening downward, solid club-shaped to wider in middle, becoming equal **Flesh:** White, slowly staining pinkish to wine-red then gradually darkening to purple-gray or blackish when exposed especially at junction between cap and stem, 2-3 cm thick **Habitat:** Under Aspen and conifers **Edibility:** Stalk may be toxic **Comments:** This species has a number of look-a-likes some of which may not be edible. Also in the Yukon. Similar to *L. insigne* which has flesh that stains bluish gray to blackish without the reddish or pinkish phase and fruit under Birch and Aspen.

Leccinum scabrum   Rough Stemmed Bolete

Cap: Pallid to tawny or yellow-brown, grayish brown or blackish brown, often developing olive tones when old, velvety to smooth, obtuse to convex, becoming plane, margin slightly inrolled to raised with age, may be somewhat tomentose and may form cracks with age, no bluish discolorations, 4-10 cm broad **Pores:** Yellowish-white turning grayish, very small, round to irregular, not staining when bruised or slowly staining yellowish, deeply depressed around stem **Spore Print:** Olive-brown **Stalk:** Whitish to grayish to blackish, with dark brown to blackish scabers, which is usually coarse in lower part of stalk and changes to fine, sometimes almost glandular squamules in the upper half, solid, widening downward, sometimes with bluish green stains near base, dry **Flesh:** Whitish turning pink then reddish and slightly violet when exposed to air; soft, not turning blue when bruised but sometimes staining slightly yellowish or ochre **Habitat:** Single, scattered or in groups in open forest on ground under hardwoods, especially Birch and also in meadows **Edibility:** There are cases of GI distress caused by members of the *L. scabrum/insigne* group. Turns black when dried or cooked. **Comments:** Also in the Yukon.

Leccinum versipelle   Orange Birch Bolete

Cap: Bright orange to bright reddish orange then dull orange with rose tinge, fading to pinkish tan when old, convex, margin with hanging remnants at first, at least when young, dry, almost bald, convex becoming broadly convex, obscurely fibrillose when young, 4-10 cm across **Pores:** Pallid or whitish to olive-buff when young, becoming dingy brown when old, bruising olive to olive-brown or darker; tube layer depressed near stem when old **Spore Print:** Brown to yellow-brown **Stalk:** Dense layer of black scabers when young and mature with a whitish background, bluish stains near base, scabers with slight flush of reddish around dark squamules, dry **Flesh:** White, staining reddish, then purple-gray to blackish when exposed, especially where stem meets cap, firm when young **Habitat:** Associated with paper and Dwarf Birch **Edibility:** Poisonous for some people **Comments:** Common in Alaska and the Yukon. Much confusion surrounds the red *Leccinums*. Formerly known as *L. testaceoscabrum.*

Sarcodon imbricatus   Hawks Wing

Fruiting Body: Buff to pale brown or dull reddish brown, convex to flat becoming sunken, darker brown with age; covered with large, coarse, broad, brown to nearly black scales that are often upturned with age and can wear off except in center; cap surface sometimes cracking when old; 5-20 cm wide **Spines:** White when young, then pale brown, becoming gray-brown to purple-brown, soft, brittle, slightly decurrent, awl-shaped, extending to margin; no bruising reaction **Spore Print:** Brownish **Stalk:** Pale brown to pinkish buff, central or off-center, more or less smooth, often enlarged in lower part, can be hollow toward top; base bulbous **Flesh:** White to brownish, grayish tan, thick, firm, but brittle, homogeneous, fleshy-fibrous **Habitat:** On ground in forests often in rows or semi circles **Edibility:** Yes, but some are bitter or spicy hot causing indigestion; must be thoroughly cooked and even then, not all that tasty, though frying thinly sliced specimens gives them a pleasant, nutty flavor. Not prone to insect infestation. A good beginner mushroom since there are no look-a-likes. Tasting, chewing and spitting out a small piece prior to collecting is a good way to tell the good from the ugly. **Comments:** Formerly known as *Hydnum dentinum* and *Hydnum imbricatum*. Also common in the Yukon.

Fomitopsis mounceae   Red-belted Conk

Fruiting Body: Brownish, with reddish and whitish belts, resinous crust, initially knob-like becoming bracket-like or hoof-shaped, appearing varnished, stemless, 5-25 cm broad **Pores:** White to yellowish, tiny, does not bruise brown Plants such as Lupine exhibit this too. **Spore Print:** White or pale yellowish **Stalk:** Absent **Flesh:** Yellowish-brown on multiple layers of pores **Habitat:** On dead or sometimes dying conifer trees, especially hemlock stumps and logs **Edibility:** It is probably toxic, reportedly causing severe gastrointestinal distress. **Comments:** Very common in Alaska and the Yukon. Formerly known as *Fomes pinicola* and *Ungulina marginata.* The conk fruits for years, adding new tube layers each year. Counting the tube layers tells you how many years the conk has been forming.

An important decomposer of conifer wood. It is mistaken for a Reishi species such as *Ganoderma lingzhi* which is not found in Alaska. *P. pinicola* was a misapplied name. *Laricifomes officinalis (*Agarikon, formerly *Fomitopsis officinalis*) is also in Alaska fruiting high up on conifers. It is hoof to column shaped with chalky white flesh. It is extremely bitter, slightly poisonous and medicinal. It is said to treat infectious diseases, including coughing illnesses, asthma, rheumatoid arthritis, bleeding, and infected wounds The mushroom was an important resource for Shamans, who would apply Agarikon powder to cure ailments thought to be caused by supernatural forces.

Laetiporus conifericola Chicken-of-the-Woods

Fruiting Body: Bright orange to salmon, margin usually yellow, fading when old to yellowish, buff or dull whitish to white, shelving, fan-shaped to elongated along wood, often uneven or wrinkled, 5-60 cm long and up to 4 cm thick **Pores:** Sulfur yellow tubes **Spore Print:** White **Stalk:** Absent or with broad lateral stem **Flesh:** Pale yellow, thick, soft, succulent and watery when fresh, when very young often exuding yellow or orange droplets, becoming tough and then crumbly or chalky white, not zoned **Habitat:** On mature conifers and hardwoods, annual, single or more often overlapping in clusters on dead stumps and logs, or on living trees or from roots **Edibility:** Edible if thoroughly cooked. Poisoning has occurred if this species is eaten raw and gets tougher and sourer with age, margin more tender than the rest of the fruiting body, associated with allergic and gastrointestinal symptoms **Comments:** This species has long been known as *L. sulphureus*, but that species has been found to include several species including *L. conifericola* characterized by habitat on conifer species. Although *L. conifericola* fruits on hardwoods as well.

Phaeolus schweinitzii   Dye Polypore

Cap: Yellow to rusty orange tones that change color with age, arranged in several tiers from common base, up to 30 cm across **Pores:** Mustard yellow to greenish turning brown or blackish when bruised **Spore Print:** White or tinged yellow to green **Stalk:** Usually tapering downward if present **Flesh:** Yellowish brown to rusty brown or brown **Habitat:** On roots and bases of trees and snags **Edibility:** Probably poisonous, but I can't imagine tasting it. Like almost all Polypores, too tough to eat. It's poisonous to trees too. **Comments:** Widespread in most states, including Alaska and the Yukon. Used to give a rich color to wool.

Artomyces pyxidatus — Crowned Coral

Fruiting Body: Whitish to pale yellow when young, to dull ochre or tinged pinkish, with multiple branches and distinctly crown-like branch tips **Spore Print:** White **Stalk:** Colored like lower branches, slender **Flesh:** Whitish, pliable, tough; odor a little like that of freshly dug potatoes **Habitat:** Fruits directly from dead wood, usually hardwoods or in moss **Edibility:** Peppery taste, somewhat edible for some but may cause gastric upset for others **Comments:** The species name means "a small box"—a reference to its branched tips. Formerly named *Clavulina pyxidata* and *Clavicorona pyxidata.* It's in the Yukon.

Ramaria formosa — Yellow-tipped Coral

Fruiting Body: Orange-red to salmon with yellow to yellowish tips, bruising brownish when handled, broadly obovate in outline, usually growing in clusters of 2-5, major branches 2-4, ascending but not erect, more or less round in cross-section, branches in 4-6 ranks, axils rounded, tips cusped when young, elongating to minutely finger-like by maturity, but remaining crowded, medium to large in size, up to 9 cm wide and up to 15 cm tall **Spore Print:** Pale ochraceous to golden yellow **Stalk:** Colored as surface or more intensely, indistinct, large, underground part white or brownish white, white-hairy at base, rounded to bluntly tapered **Flesh:** Pinkish-orange to light red or salmon, in branches, solid, pastel, rosy orange under spore-bearing surface; in stem, solid, soft, moist but not slippery, fleshy, somewhat spongy at base when fresh, drying brittle and very chalky-friable **Habitat:** On ground under conifers **Edibility:** Poisonous, reported to cause diarrhea or gastric upset **Comments:** Common in Alaska and the Yukon.

Ascomycetes

Helvella crispa
White Fluted Elfin Saddle

Cap: Yellowish to creamy white, fuzzy on underside of cap; when young margins rolled up over spore-bearing surface, saddle-shaped to irregularly lobed when mature, 2-5 cm tall **Spores:** Elliptical; smooth with a large, central oil droplet and sometimes, several smaller droplets at each end **Stalk:** Same color as cap, ornately fluted, fuzzy, chambered, often with holes in surface **Flesh:** Thin, elastic, brittle **Habitat:** On ground in hardwood and coniferous forests, uncommon **Edibility:** To be avoided as it has caused gastric upsets in some people **Comments:** A spore shooter that fires its spores out from its cap rather than drop them from below the cap. Another Alaskan species is *H. elastica* the Smooth Stem Elfin Saddle. As its name implies, it has a smooth rather than fluted often white stem. It is to be avoided. *Helvellas* are sometimes listed as edible but some can cause upset stomachs and research shows some to be carcinogenic. Not suitable for the table.

Helvella vespertina Black Fluted Elfin Saddle

Cap: Dark brown to gray or gray-black, convex, saddle-shaped to conical, very lobed, wrinkled and twisted, upper surface smooth, irregularly chambered, thin-walled, tough, margin attached to stalk at several places, 4-7 cm high, 3-5 cm broad **Spores:** Elliptical with 1 oil droplet **Stalk:** Grayish, deeply fluted or ribbed with grooved and ridged interior chamber **Flesh:** Thin, brittle, gray-black to black **Habitat:** Solitary, clustered or scattered on ground or on decaying wood under coniferous and deciduous trees **Edibility:** Avoid. It is eaten but not recommended due to its similarity to the deadly poisonous *Gyromitra infula* (False Morel) **Comments:** Also known as *H. lacunosa* and found in the Yukon.

Gyromitra esculenta Brain Mushroom

Cap: Brownish to golden or reddish-brown, somewhat round, brain-like, not conspicuously lobed, lobes separated by deep furrows, 5-11 cm broad, 5-9 cm tall **Spores:** Pale yellow in deposit, elliptical, smooth, with 2 oil droplets requiring a microscope to see

Stalk: Whitish often tinged vinaceous-tan, round to compressed, sometimes grooved or with basal folds, unbranched, often fluted, scruffy to almost smooth **Flesh:** Interior chambered, brittle, odor nor distinctive **Habitat:** On ground, solitary to scattered under conifers **Edibility:** Deadly including the fumes **Comments:** Found world-wide including Alaska and the Yukon. Formerly known as *Helvella esculenta*; contains mono-methyl-hydrazine (see comments under next species). The species name *esculata* means edible as the toxins can be removed by parboiling or drying and rehydrating which does not always remove all toxins. Not at all recommended for eating! Another poisonous False Morel in Alaska is *Gyromitra ambigua*. Even consumption of the water used in boiling the fungus apparently resulted in a poisonous reaction. The cap is red-brown to dark red brown, often with violet tints. It is saddle-shaped or 2-lobed (like the Hooded False Morel) to irregularly lobed. *G. gigas* is another species found in the alpine and tundra of Alaska. It is also contains monomethylhydrazine.

Gyromitra infula — Hooded False Morel

Cap: Reddish to dark brown, saddle-shaped usually 2 sometimes 3-4 lobed, cup-shaped when very young, with two or three lobes on short stalk, irregularly bumpy but not wrinkled, small, 3-9 cm broad, 3-8 cm tall **Spores:** Oblong-elliptical, smooth, typically with two large microscopic oil droplets **Stalk:** Colored like cap or paler, smooth to minutely velvety, not ribbed but can be grooved **Flesh:** Colored like cap or lighter, thin, brittle **Habitat:** Under conifers or hardwoods, and on recently burned sites in the Interior **Edibility:** Deadly especially when eaten raw, contains the chemical gyromitrin which becomes monomethylhydrazine (MMH), a toxic and carcinogenic compound used to make rocket fuel. Breathing fumes from cooking can be lethal **Comments:** Formerly known as *Helvella infula* which makes sense as it can be confused with *Helvella vespertina*, (aka *H. lacunosa*) but this *Helvella* has darker caps and deeply fluted stalks. For accurate identification, spore examination under a microscope is necessary. *Gyromitra* species have two oil droplets, *Helvella* species have one. *G. esculenta* fruits in spring while *G. infula* fruits in late summer and fall. *Helvellas* have non-fluted, usually more slender stems and the cap color is generally different. These species are difficult to tell apart. Don't eat them.

Morchella sextelata   Black Morel

Cap: Dull brownish to yellowish tan background, ridge tips black, conic to widely conic, pits and ridges are mostly vertically oriented; ridge surface bald or finely tomentose; 2-5 cm across, 3-9 cm tall **Stalk:** Whitish, bald or finely mealy with granules, can be chambered near base; hollow **Flesh:** Whitish **Habitat:** Fruits in recently burned conifer forests **Edibility:** *Morchella*s are generally considered choice edibles, but *M. sextelata* has been implicated in a mass mushroom poisoning which sickened 51 people and resulted in 3 hospitalizations and 2 deaths. **Comments:** This species was first described in 2012. Possibly saprobic on soil and leaf mold and mycorrhizal at different points in its life cycle.

Verpa bohemica   Early Morel

Cap: Yellowish to reddish-brown, somewhat bell-shaped, attached to stem only at apex, margin free from stem, surface prominently ridged with reticulations **Spores:** Large, thin-walled, smooth **Stalk:** Whitish, becoming yellow with age, smooth, cottony at base **Flesh:** Thin, fragile, usually with wispy fibers similar to cotton candy **Habitat:** Single or in groups on ground in mixed wood, especially under large Cottonwoods **Edibility:** Edible, but should be tested if eaten for the first time. There are reports of mild to severe and cumulative poisoning. Do not eat raw **Comments:** Common in Alaska and Yukon. Formerly known as *V. bispora.* Also included in *Edible Mushrooms of Alaska.*

Cudonia circinans   Curled Cudonia

Cap: Cream-buff to pale brownish, cushion-shaped to irregularly convex, sometimes with a shallow depression, margin curled under, smooth or somewhat wrinkled, .5-2 cm broad **Spores:** Needle-shaped, smooth, septate **Stalk:** Brownish, finely fuzzy or smooth, can have ridges that extend to undersurface of cap **Flesh:** Thin, insubstantial but not gelatinous **Habitat:** In clusters, gregariously or scattered on conifer duff **Edibility:** Poisonous, contains gyromitrin **Comments:** Found throughout Alaska and the Yukon. A related species, *Spathularia flavida* is flattened, spoon-shaped and found on mosses under white or Black Spruce and is of unknown edibility.

This is the second book in the four part *Mushrooms of Alaska* series. It covers the least number of species than any other book in the series. This is good. It means there are more edible and common than poisonous fungi in Alaska! The final book is a compilation of all species I have found and/or documented in Alaska and the Yukon: *Fungi and Other Mushrooms of Alaska.*

REFERENCES

Alaska's Mushrooms: A Wide-Ranging Guide Gary Laursen and Neil McArthur

Common Interior Alaska Cryptogams Gary Laursen and Rodney D. Seppelt

Mushrooms of the National Forests of Alaska USDA Steve Trudell and Kate Mohatt.

Mushrooms of the Pacific Northwest Steve Trudell and Joe Ammirati, There is also a revised edition.

Alaska's Mushrooms: A Practical Guide (Alaska Pocket Guide) Harriette Parker

Mushrooms of British Columbia, Royal BC Museum Handbook, Andy MacKinnon and Kem Luther

Mushrooms of the Pacific Northwest (on-line) www.matchmakermushrooms.com
A fantastic reference put together by Ian Gibson

Mushrooms Demystified and *All That the Rain Promises and More: A Hip Pocket Guide to Western Mushrooms* David Arora

Ascomycete Fungi of North America Michael Beug, Alan Bessette and Arleen Bessette

Mushrooms of Northwest North America Helene Schalkwijk-Barendsen

North American Boletes A Color Guide to the Fleshy Pored Mushrooms Alan E. Bessette, William C. Roody and Arleen R. Bessette

Native Plants of Southeast Alaska Windy Ridge Press. Judy Hall

Giant Polypores & Stoned Reindeer: Rambles in the Kingdom Fungi Lawrence Millman
and......
Facebook Pages: Mushrooms and other Fungi of Alaska and **Alaska Mushrooms**

You can NEVER have too many mushroom books!

GLOSSARY

Adnate: gills broadly attached (perpendicular) to the stem

Adnexed: gills narrowly attached to the stem apex

Annulus: a ring or skirt-like partial veil surrounding the stem

Apex: tip

Asci: the cell in which karyogamy and meiosis occurs and in which spores are formed in the *Ascomycetes*

Ascospores: the spore produced and contained within the ascus of an *Ascomycete* fungi; the ascus typically contains eight ascospores; the ascospores are formed by meiotic and mitotic divisions

Appressed: pressed closely or fitting closely to something

Ascomycete: one of the *Ascomycota*, a phylum of fungi that produce asci and ascospores

Basidia: the cell in which karyogamy and meiosis occurs and in which spores are formed in the *Basidiomycota*

Basidiomycete: one of the *Basidiomycota*, a phylum of fungi that produce basidia and basidiospores

Caespitose: when a mushroom grows in dense clusters, with the stems fused together or packed right up against one another at the base

Companulate: bell-shaped

Convex: curving outward, rounded

Coprine: an amino acid which interacts negatively with alcohol in the human body exacerbating the worst symptoms of alcohol intoxication

Cortina: a thin, web-like veil extending from the edge of the cap to the stalk common in the genus *Cortinarius*

Decurrent: gills running down the stem

Deliquescing: when a mushroom melts away, often turning black, in the course of growth or decay

Disc: the center of the cap

Emarginate gill: when a gill has roughly the same height for most of its length, then suddenly becomes much shallower just before reaching the stem

Evanescent: soon disappearing

Fibrillous: covered with silk-like fibers

Floccus: delicately cottony

Free Gills: none of the gills connect to the stem

Fulvous: tawny; dull yellow, with a mixture of gray and brown

Furfuraceous: covered with minute bran-like particles, scurfy

Gills: radiating, spore bearing structures on which spores are produced

Glabrous: lacking ornamentation, not hairy.

Granulose: surface covered with small granules

Hygrophanous: changing color with moisture loss

Hymenium: the spore-bearing layer of a fruiting body

Hypha: one of the filaments of a fungus

Inrolled: incurved or rolled inwards

Karyogamy: the final step in the process of fusing together two haploid eukaryotic cells and refers specifically to the fusion of the two nuclei

KOH: Potassium Hydroxide, used in the identification of many mushrooms, including boletes, polypores, and gilled mushrooms; they change color with a drop of KOH

Lamellae: the scientific term for gills

Liliaceous: having elongated parts that grow from a corm, bulb, or rhizome

Meiosis: the process of cell division in sexually reproducing organisms that reduces the number of chromosomes in reproductive cells from diploid to haploid

Melzer's reagent: an iodine, potassium iodide and chloral hydrate solution used in microscopic analysis

Mushroom: a fungal fruiting body, especially one that fruits in a short period of time as opposed to one such as a conk, that is hard and inedible and grows over years

Muscarine: is a natural product found in certain mushrooms, particularly in *Inocybe* and *Clitocybe* species; such as the deadly *C. dealbata*. Mushrooms in the genera *Entoloma* and *Mycena* have also been found to contain levels of muscarine which can be dangerous if ingested. Muscarine is found in harmless trace amounts in *Boletus, Hygrocybe, Lactarius* and *Russula*. Muscarine, originally isolated in *Amanita muscaria*, is only a trace compound in the Fly Agaric; the pharmacologically more relevant compound from this mushroom is muscimol.

Mycelium: a mass of hyphae; the mostly below ground, vegetative part of a fungus

Mycophobia: the irrational fear of mushrooms

Mycorrhiza: symbiotic, nonpathogenic, or weakly pathogenic association of a fungus and the roots of a plant

Notched: refers to gills of many *Tricholoma* species; similar to emarginate

Obovate: ovate with the narrower end at the base

Ovate: having an outline like a longitudinal section of an egg with the basal end broader

Ochraceous: brownish-yellow; of the color of ocher

Obtuse: having a rounded or blunt tip

Oil Drops: Ascospores mounted in KOH sometimes show "oil droplets," and the number and disposition of the droplets are taxonomically important.

Pallid: pale

Partial veil: temporary structure of tissue extending from the margin of the cap to the stem found on the fruiting bodies of some basidiomycete fungi, typically agarics. Also called an inner veil, to differentiate it from the outer veil

Peel: the skin of the cap

Pellicle: the thin outer layer of a mushroom cap

Phylum: the taxonomic classification above Family

Pileus: the cap of the mushroom with the hymanium-supporting part of the fruiting body

Planoconvex: with one surface flat and the opposite one convex

Phenolic: an odor that is unpleasant and tar-like, in mushrooms such as *Agaricus*

Polypore: a tough fruiting body with poroid spore-bearing surface

Pubescent: having soft hairs

Punctate: pitted

Rhizomorphs: a rootlike aggregation of hypae

Reticulations: a raised network pattern

Scabers: rough, scabrous little scurfy things that stick up on members of the genus *Leccinum*

Sinuate: gill being roughly the same height for most of its length, becoming much shallower and then curving back towards the stem before reaching the attachment point

Spore print: the deposit of spores obtained by placing a mushroom cap on a sheet of paper or glass

Squamules: small scales

Squamulose: with small scales

Squarrose: Having rough or spreading scale-like processes

Stipe: stalk of a mushroom

Stuffed: stalk stuffed with a pith

Striate: marked with delicate lines, grooves or ridges

Subdecurrent: gills attached to and running downward along a stalk or stipe, but curving inward just before the attachment point

Subdistant: gills that are not quite distant, but not close either

Tomentose: having a covering of soft, matted hairs, downy

Umbo: a broad outgrowth in middle of the top of the cap

Umbonate: having an umbo

Undulate: wavy

Universal veil: a layer of tissue that encloses the entire emerging mushroom; some or all of the tissue disappears as the mushroom grows and expands

Viscid: slimy, sticky

Volva: the remnants of the universal veil on the base of the stem; often sac-like or of annular rings

Zonate: having concentric lines often forming alternating pale and darker zones

Index

Field Notes

Field Notes

www.ingramcontent.com/pod-product-compliance
Lightning Source LLC
Chambersburg PA
CBHW040952310526
45796CB00011B/1